Materials: Indian Cloth #1100 DMC Embroidery thread Size #25   Instructions on page 46

Small Flowers in a Flower Garden

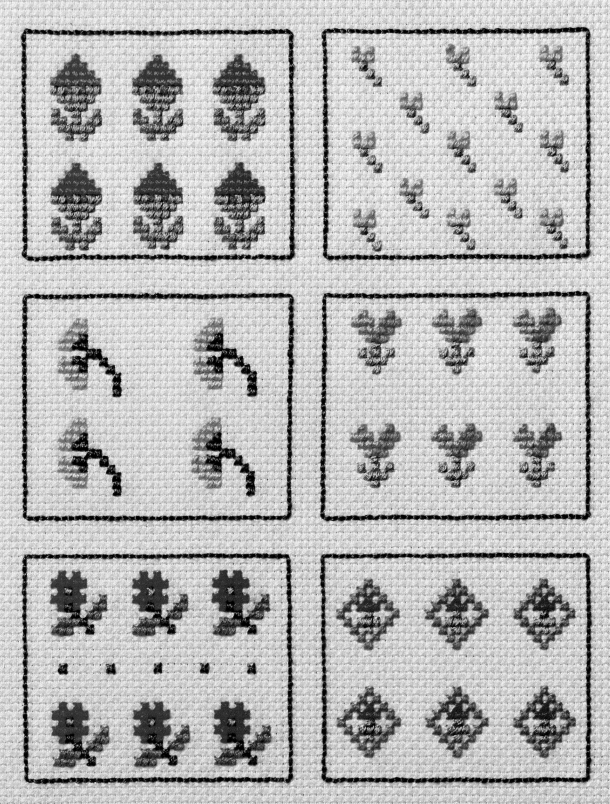

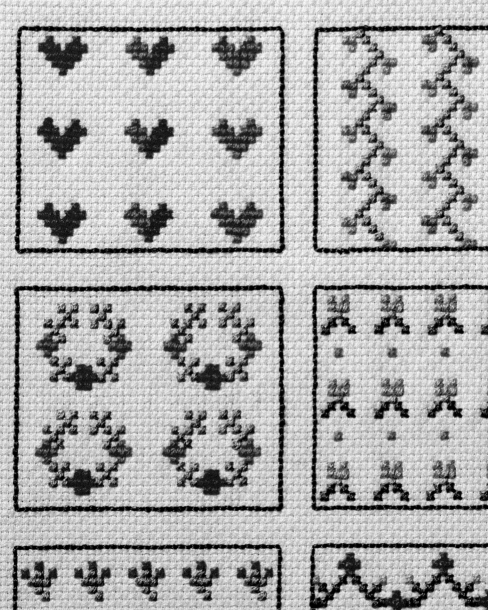

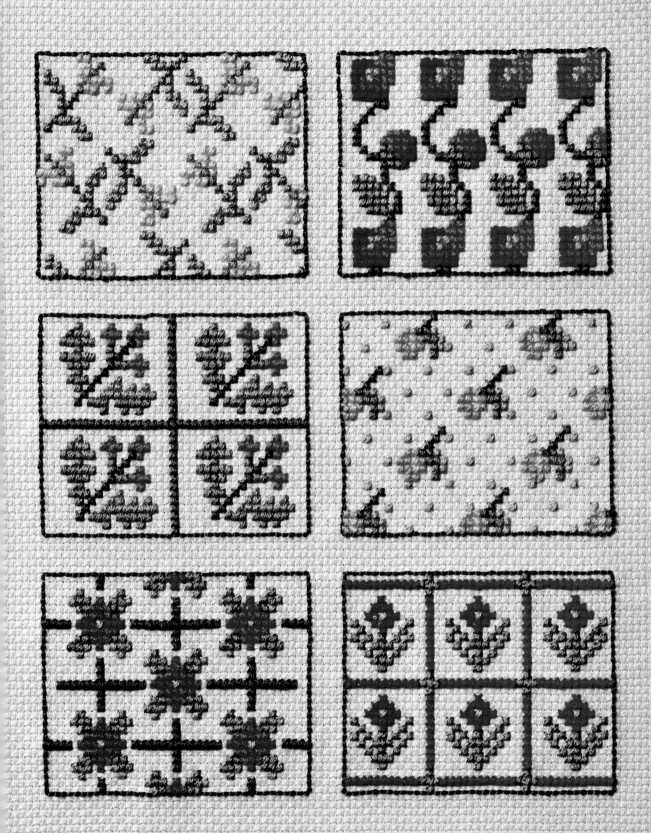

Materials: Indian Cloth #1100 DMC Embroidery thread Size #25   Instructions on page 49

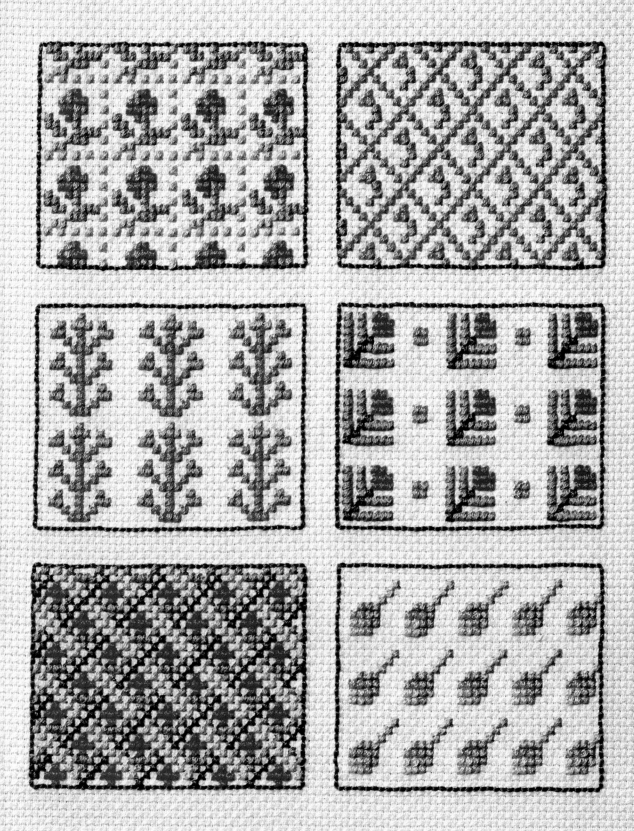

★ Applying the flower pattern to ready
   made articles

Small Pretty Flowers

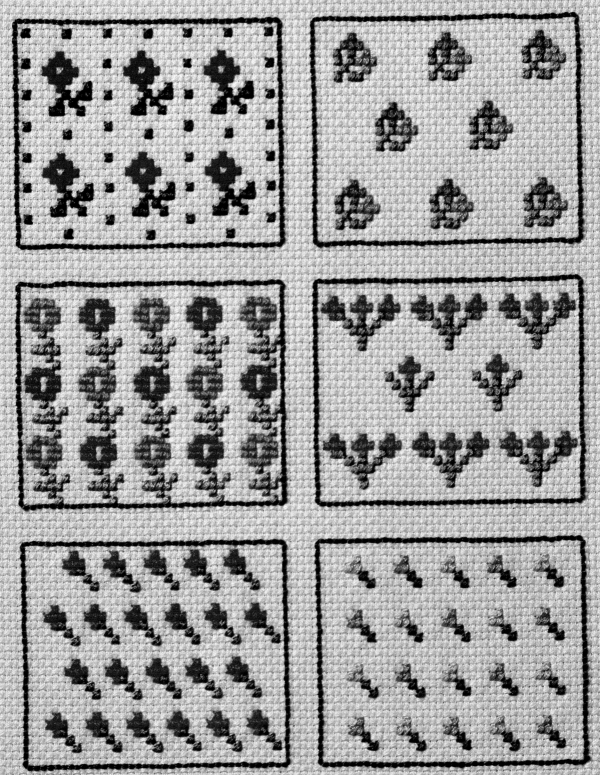

Materials: Indian Cloth #1100 DMC Embroidery thread Size #25   Instructions on page 51

Dress, Purse and Socks for a three-year-old girl

Dry Flowers

Materials: Java Cloth Fine Weave #3800 DMC Embroidery thread Size #25   Instructions on page 52

11

Flower Garden in the Breeze

★ Using the dancing flower pattern on cushions, covers for jam jars, coasters, napkin rings, and a round table-cloth

Dancing Flowers

CUSHION

Cushion wtih poppy flower   Instructions on page 56

Materials: Java Cloth Fine Weave #3800
DMC Embroidery thread Size #25   Instructions on page 56

15

TABLE CLOTH

Tablecloth

Instructions on page 58

COASTER

Coasters, covers for jam jars, and napkin rings   Instructions on page 58

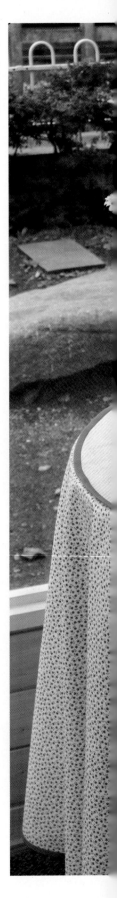

16

Lovely Flowers

Materials: Java Cloth Fine Weave #3800 DMC Embroidery thread Size #25   Instructions on page 59

Roses

Materials: Java Cloth Fine Weave #3800 DMC Embroidery thread Size #25   Instructions on page 62

21

★ The rose pattern on doily and centerpiece

DOILY

Doily
Instructions on page 61

CENTERPIECE

Centerpiece   Instructions on page 61

23

★ The small patterns used on place mats, square
  tablecloth, and tea cozy

Fairy Tales and Tiny Flowers

Materials: Indian Cloth #1100 DMC Embroidery thread Size #25   Instructions on page 64

Tablecloth and
tea cozy
Instructions on
page 66

Tree Scenes

Materials: Indian Cloth #1100 DMC Embroidery thread Size #25   Instructions on page 68

29

Sweet Flowers

CUSHION

Cushions (three types)
Instructions on page 70

Materials: Java Cloth Medium Weave
#3500 DMC Embroidery thread Size
#25 Instructions on page 71

30

Birds and Berries

Materials: Java Cloth Fine Weave #3800 DMC Embroidery thread Size #25   Instructions on page 72

32

Birds and Flowers

Materials: Java Cloth Medium Weave #3500 DMC Embroidery thread Size #25   Instructions on page 74

Patterned Checks

Materials: Indian Cloth #1100 DMC Embroidery thread Size #25   Instructions on page 76

36

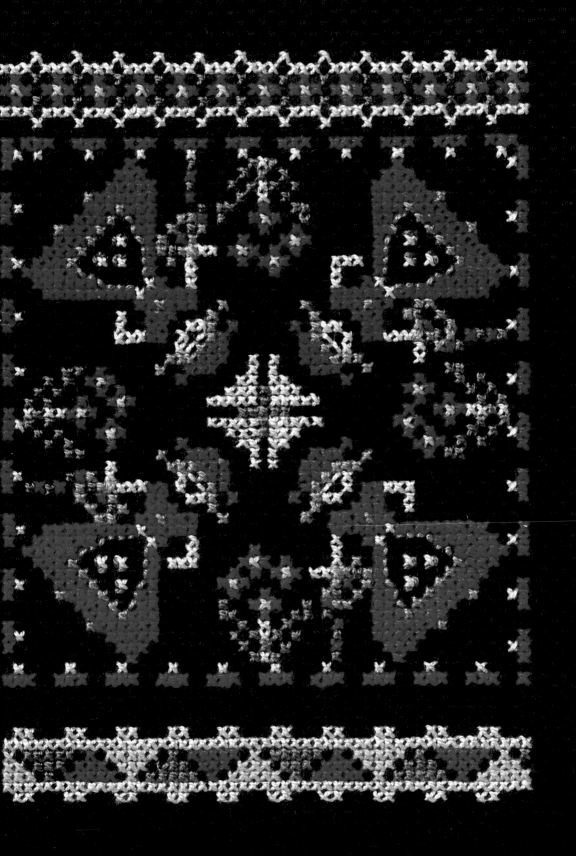

Tyrolean Patterns

Materials: opposite page: Java Cloth Medium Weave #3500 DMC Embroidery thread Size #5
this page: Java Cloth Fine Weave #3800 DMC Embroidery thread Size #25
Instructions: For opposite page: page 78   For this page: page 79

39

Continuous Pattern of Birds and Flowers

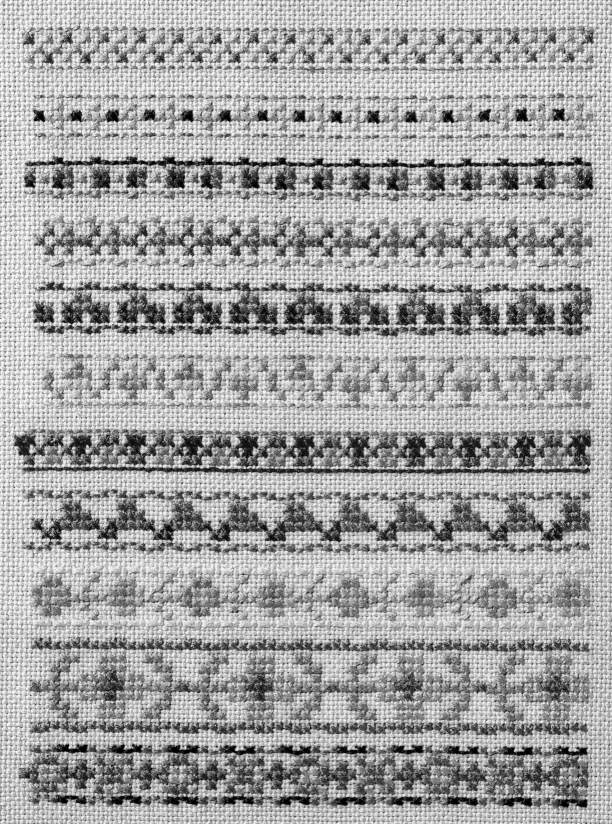

Materials: Congress Cloth #9000 DMC Embroidery thread Size #25   Instructions on page 81

41

★ The camellia pattern on a pouch bag

Camellia

POUCH

Pouch Bag   Instructions on page 82

Materials: Java Cloth Medium Weave #3500 DMC Embroidery thread Size #25
Scale of the photograph: eight-tenths of actual size   Instructions on page 82

BASIC'S OF CROSS-STITCH

Cross-stitch is historic embroidery dating back to the Byzantine empire. First introduced to Europe in Italy, it has become popular throughout the world. Cross-stitch consists of counting the squares and making one cross in each square. It is important that each stitch is crossed in the same direction.

Fabrics:

You can use any kind of material for cross-stitch. However, even-weave fabrics, which are easy to count and sew, are recommended. The five types of embroidery fabrics listed below are used for the projects in this book.

Choose a fabric to match the project. As the size of pattern varies with the size of the square of the fabric, make sure of the layout of the pattern by counting the squares; then mark the fabric before you start.

● Photographs: actual size

Indian Cloth	Java Cloth Fine Weave	Java Cloth Medium Weave	Java Cloth Large Weave	Congress
10 cm^2 50×50 sqs.	10 cm^2 45×45 sqs.	10 cm^2 35×35 sqs.	10 cm^2 25×25 sqs.	10 cm^2 67 x 67 sqs.
15 cm^2 75×75 sqs.	15 cm^2 67×67 sqs.	15 cm^2 52 x 52 sqs.	15 cm^2 37×37 sqs.	15 cm^2 100×100 sqs.
20 cm^2 100×100 sqs.	20 cm^2 90×90 sqs.	20 cm^2 70 x 70 sqs.	20 cm^2 50×50 sqs.	20 cm^2 134×134 sqs.
25 cm^2 125×125 sqs.	25 cm^2 112×112 sqs.	25 cm^2 87 x 87 sqs.	25 cm^2 62×62 sqs.	25 cm^2 167×167 sqs.
30 cm^2 150×150 sqs.	30 cm^2 135×135 sqs.	30 cm^2 105 x 105 sqs.	30 cm^2 75×75 sqs.	30 cm^2 201×201 sqs.
35 cm^2 175×175 sqs.	35 cm^2 157×157 sqs.	35 cm^2 122 x 122 sqs.	35 cm^2 87×87 sqs.	35 cm^2 234×234 sqs.
40 cm^2 200×200 sqs.	40 cm^2 180×180 sqs.	40 cm^2 140 x 140 sqs.	40 cm^2 100×100 sqs.	40 cm^2 268×268 sqs.
50 cm^2 250×250 sqs.	50 cm^2 225×225 sqs.	50 cm^2 175 x 175 sqs.	50 cm^2 125×125 sqs.	50 cm^2 335×335 sqs.

Threads and Needles

Threads:

Embroidery thread sizes #25 and #5 are usually used for cross-stitch. Thread size #25 consists of six thin strands twined loosely. You can use two or three strands or gather nine or twelve strands, according to the type of fabric or stitch.

Needles:

Needles for cross-stitch have round points and their sizes range from #19 to #23. The larger the number, the smaller the needle. Choose needles according to the thickness of the thread.

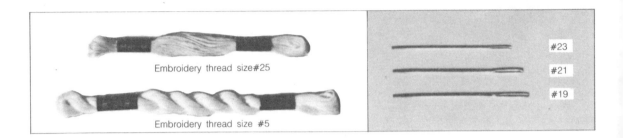

Embroidery thread size#25

Embroidery thread size #5

#23
#21
#19

Needle	Threads		Fabric				
	#25	#5					
#19	5 or 6 strands	1 strand			Java cloth (Medium)	Java cloth (Large)	
#21	3 or 4 strands		Indian cloth	Java cloth (Fine)			Congress (2×2 sqs.)
#23	2 strands						

Basic Cross-Stitch

Working one stitch at a time:

Bring needle out and make half-stitch from top left (#1) to bottom right (#2) and work back over this stitch as shown (#3–4). This completes one stitch. Note that the second cross is a top stitch.

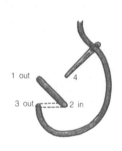

1 out
4
3 out
2 in

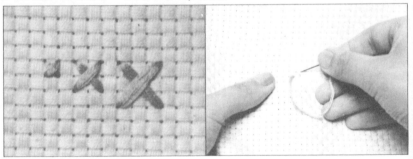

Working across to complete rows:

Make one stitch at a time as described above. Continue horizontally from right to left, as shown.

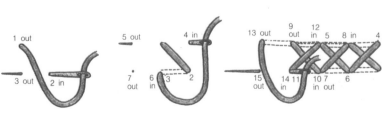

1 out
3 out
2 in

5 out
4 in
7 out
6 in
3
2

13 out
9 out
12 in
5
8 in
4
15 out
14 in
11
10 7
in out
6

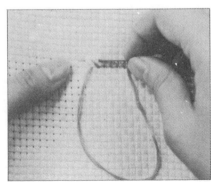

Working vertically to complete rows:

Make half-stitches from top to bottom. Work back over these stitches as shown.

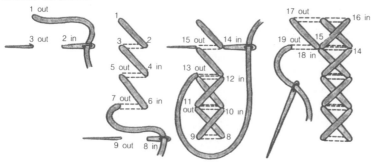

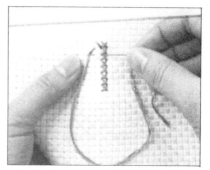

Working diagonally from bottom right to top left:

Make one cross-stitch at a time. Continue diagonally from bottom right to top left as shown.

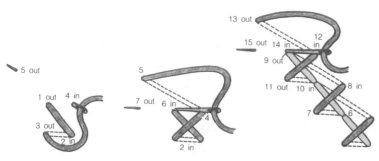

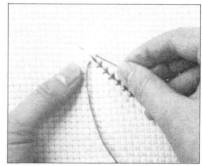

Working diagonally from top right to bottom left:

Make one cross-stitch at a time. Continue diagonally from top right to bottom left as shown.

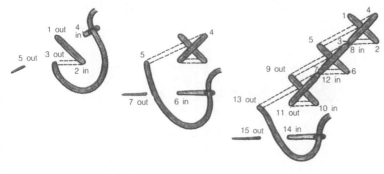

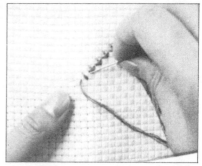

Finishing & Hemstitching:

Place the fabric on the back of cross-stitch and sew as shown in diagrams 1–3. Work from left to right.

How to hemstitch (Back)

Finished Diagram (Front)

①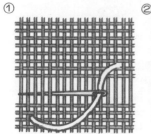

②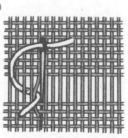

③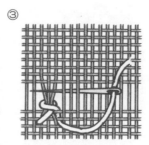

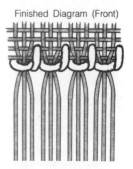

Flower Garden

(Shown on page 2)

▼	#915 dark red violet	/	#718 dark pink	✎	#326 red	▲	#433 dark brown
✕	#699 green	∧	#993 light blue green	○	#893 pink	∅	#210 light purple
◣	#937 dark green	⊙	#946 orange	●	#834 pale yellow		

+ #334 blue

‖ #704 yellow green

∨ #601 dark violet

L #718 violet

● #915 dark violet

□ #733 olive

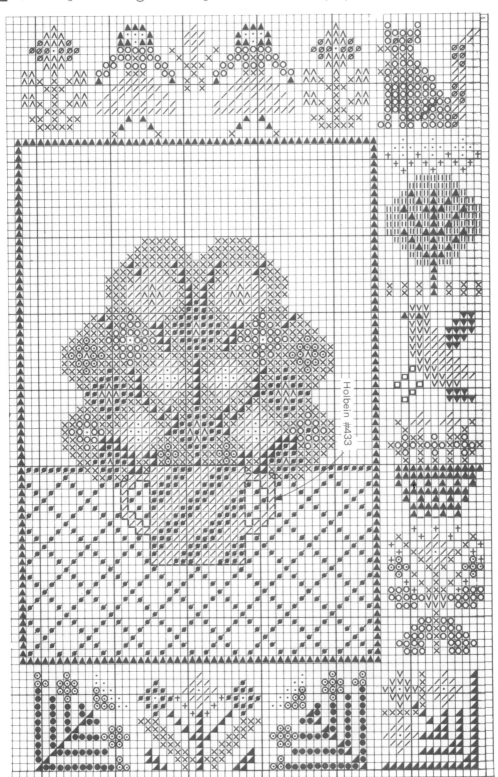

Holbein #433

Small Flowers in a Flower Garden

(Shown on pages 4 to 7)

Shown on page 4

=	#718	dark and light
+	#915	purple red
⊘	#910	green
◣	#312	blue
⊥	#743	bright yellow
\	#3354	pale pink

●	#935	dark moss green
–	#312	dark and light
V	#498	red
○	#205	iris purple
●	#702	yellow green
▲	#470	pale green

//	#893	pink
▽	#740	dark and light
X	#946	orange

The square outlines around flowers are to be worked in Holbein stitch using dark moss green (#935).

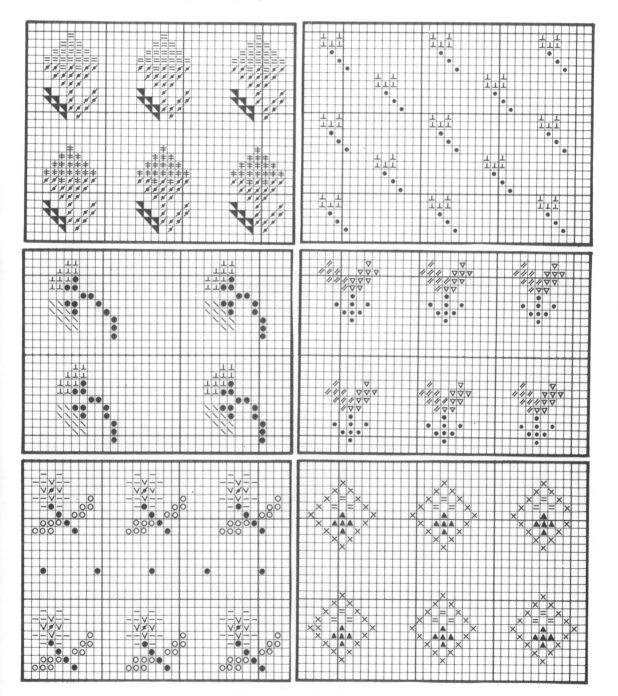

47

Shown on page 5

/   #602   dark pink
▲   #946   orange
✕   #702   yellow green
○   #899   light pink
●   #718   light purple
V   #993   sky blue
■   #730   olive

The square outlines around flowers are to be worked in Holbein stitch using dark moss green (#935).

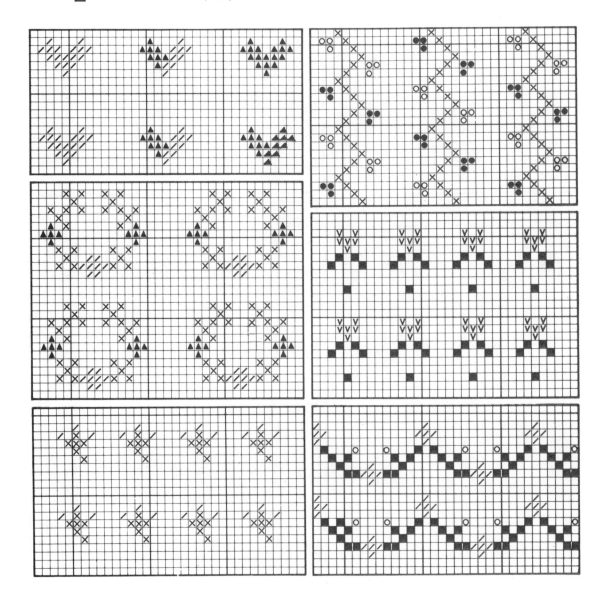

48

Shown on page 6

🐦	#907		
✕	#703	shades of	
V	#701	yellow green	
●	#700		
△	#733		
T	#731	shades of olive	
●	#730		
■	#209	wisteria	

⊙	#947	dark orange
∴	#518	greenish blue
=	#3346	light and dark pale green
◤	#895	
◣	#915	
‖	#917	shades of violet
▲	#718	
＼	#603	

+	#640	grayish brown
⊥	#309	violet
<	#817	red
//	#801	dark brown
↗	#3327	pale red
○	#307	yellow

The square outlines around flowers are to be worked in Holbein stitch using dark moss green (#935).

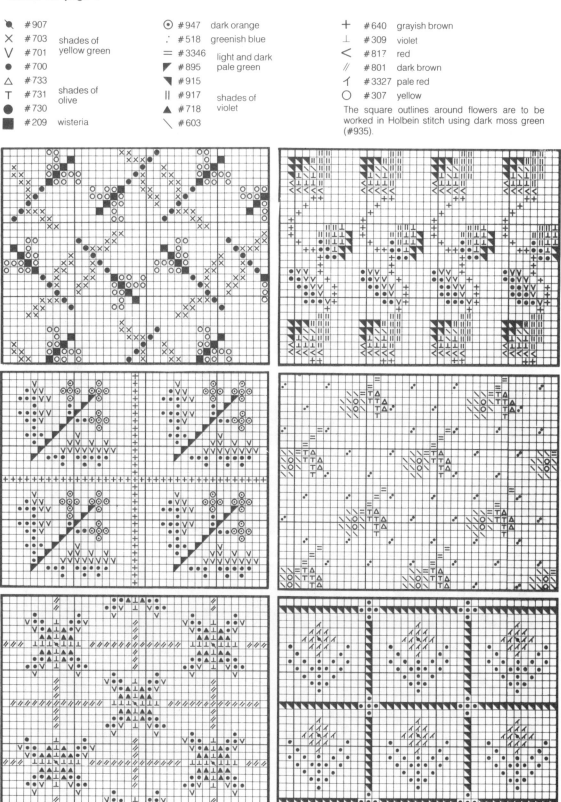

49

Shown on page 7

T #992 sky blue
⊙ #991 light green
O #793 light pale blue
V #718 purple red
◣ #907 light yellow green
/ #704 yellow green

✕ #798 blue
◢ #703 light yellow green
◼ #730 olive
‖ #892 dark pink
● #701 green

The square outlines around flowers are to be worked in Holbein stitch using dark moss green (#935).

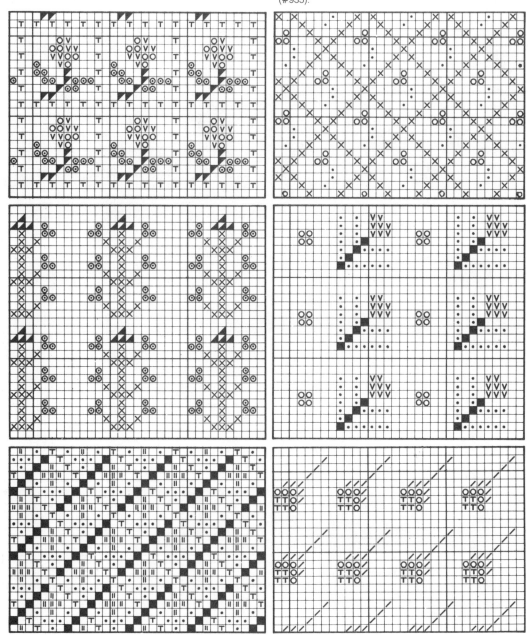

Small Pretty Flowers

(Shown on pages 8 and 9)

Shown on page 8

X	#701	light and dark
●	#703	yellow green
/	#604	
T	#602	shades of
≋	#601	violet
○	#600	

+	#935	dark olive
◣	#3346	dark green
−	#718	light and dark
V	#915	red violet
⊙	#992	very light green
T	#209	wisteria
◢	#844	dark gray

▽	#211	
⊥	#210	shades of wisteria
●	#208	
■	#444	yellow

Four strands are used for the stitches on page 9.
Determine the number of strands by the type of fabric.

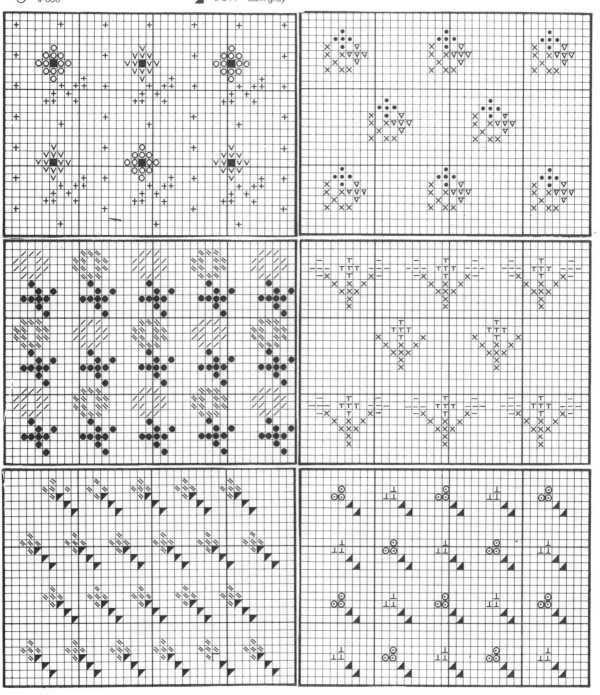

51

Dry Flowers

(Shown on pages 10 and 11)

Shown on page 10

Symbol	Code	Name
⚲	#891	salmon
◤	#602	light red violet
⬙	#666	red
⬛	#632	light brown
◢	#741	yellow orange
⦀	#743	bright yellow
▽	#991	blue green
▲	#907	yellow green
/	#906	dark olive
▬	#829	dark olive
▼	#604	shades of violet
⊙	#917	shades of violet
=	#915	
T	#208	wisteria
‖	#600	red violet
+	#704	
☐	#701	shades of green
×	#700	shades of green
●	#703	
○	#831	olive
※	#798	blue

52

X	#700	+	#604	○	#600
◎	#907	⊥	#917 shades of red violet	✿	#602 shades of violet
◢	#937	‖	#915	V	#603
●	#3343 shades of green	T	#208 wisteria	=	#604
∧	#912	■	#632 light brown	/	#322 blue
□	#832	.·	#839 dark brown	▽	#791 pale blue
●	#470	—	#726 yellow	⊙	#970 orange

Flower Garden in the Breeze

(Shown on pages 12 and 13)

Shown on page 12

V	#605	shades of red violet
—	#603	
T	#602	
⊙	#970	light and dark orange
▲	#946	
+	#907	shades of yellow green
✕	#905	
/	#702	
⧅	#700	
∴	#471	
●	#992	light green
■	#839	dark brown
∧	#604	shades of violet
●	#602	
○	#600	

54

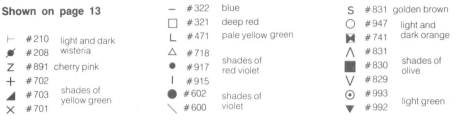

Shown on page 13

⊢	#210	light and dark wisteria	—	#322	blue	S	#831	golden brown
✿	#208		□	#321	deep red	○	#947	light and dark orange
Z	#891	cherry pink	L	#471	pale yellow green	◪	#741	
+	#702		△	#718	shades of red violet	∧	#831	shades of olive
◢	#703	shades of yellow green	●	#917		■	#830	
			∣	#915		V	#829	
×	#701		●	#602	shades of violet	⊙	#993	light green
			＼	#600		▼	#992	

Dancing Flowers

(Shown on pages 14 to 17)

∧	#912	
⫽	#704	
○	#906	shades of green
◢	#369	
✕	#3346	
■	#890	
∅	#352	peach
T	#315	mauve
◑	#666	red
=	#783	golden brown
◖	#906	olive
−	#301	red brown
∟	#839	dark brown
╲	#741	bright yellow
⊙	#744	yellow
△	#809	light blue
V	#798	blue
I	#995	sky blue
●	#310	black
+	#817	light and dark salmon
╱	#351	

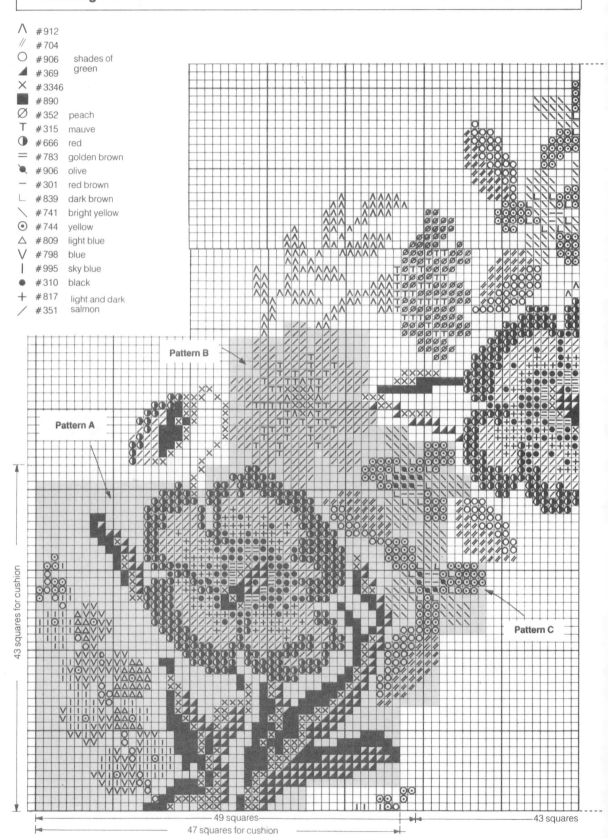

Pattern B

Pattern A

Pattern C

43 squares for cushion

49 squares

47 squares for cushion

43 squares

56

Cushion

Materials: Java cloth medium weave white (#11) 91×50 cm; DMC embroidery thread size #25: 2 skeins of red #666, one skein each of colors designated on page 56 and dark yellow #725. Inner bag 91×50 cm; filling 400g; 40-cm white zipper.

Finished size: See the diagram.

Instructions: 18 squares from the center, make two square patterns in dark yellow #783, referring to chart. In each of the four quarters, work pattern A as in the following diagram, using six strands for each color. When finished, complete cushion as in diagram below.

Center part of cushion

Finished diagram

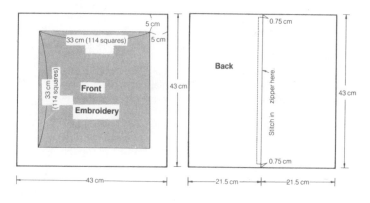

Cover for Jam Jars

Materials (for one piece): Java cloth fine weave white (#11) 16 x 16 cm; White lining 16×16 cm; DMC embroidery thread size #25: red #666, light brown #840, blue #791, light blue #996 and others. Ribbon tape in the same color as the flower (8mm wide) 60 cm; white cotton lace (2 cm wide) 90 cm.

Finished size: See the diagram.

Instructions: Work pattern B in the center, using 4 strands for each color. Work to the edge; sew on cotton lace. Diameter of the jar coverlet is 13 cm. Make six loops for tape.

Coaster

Materials (for one piece): Congress red (#18) 16×16cm; DMC embroidery thread size #25: four colors for pattern B (color of petals of your choice).

Finished size: See the diagram.

Instructions: Work pattern B, starting from the center of the fabric with 4 strands for each color. Make one stitch in four squares of the fabric. Make the fringe by picking up three vertical threads at a time and finish by cutting the threads to 3 cm length.

Napkin Rings

Materials (for one piece): Congress white (#11) 20 x 10 cm; White lining 20×10 cm; DMC embroidery thread size #25: 7 colors for the flowers and leaves of pattern C; bias tape grayish green 45 cm; one snap fastener.

Finished size: See the diagram.

Instructions: Work pattern C, using four strands for each color. Make one stitch in four squares of the fabric. Sew the outer fabric and lining together, piping the border with bias tape as in the diagram below, and complete with the snap fastener.

Diagrams of finished covers for jam jars, coasters and napkin rings.

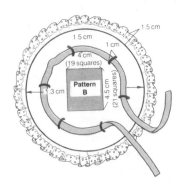

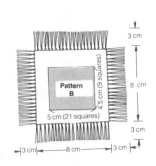

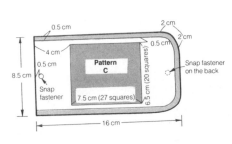

Round Tablecloth

Materials: Java cloth medium weave white (#11) 90×90 cm; DMC embroidery thread size #25: colors designated on pages 56 and 57; 5 skeins of red #666, 4 skeins of salmon pink #350, two skeins each of green #912, #3348, #906, #3346, #368, #319, yellow #725, and peach #760, one skein each of other colors; bias tape, grayish green 250 cm.

Finished size: See the diagram.

Instructions: The pattern on pages 14 and 15 is worked four times successively in a circle. First, mark the center of the fabric and then work each pattern four times clockwise. Use six strands for each color. When finished, cut the fabric into a round shape and complete by piping the edge with a bias tape. The tablecloth on page 17, made of a flower print cotton with a diameter of 180 cm, is also completed by piping the edge with the grayish green bias tape.

Diagram of finished round tablecloth

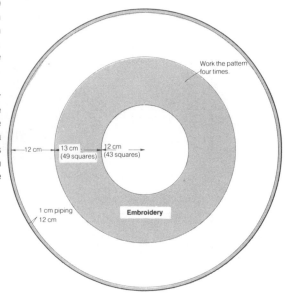

Lovely Flowers

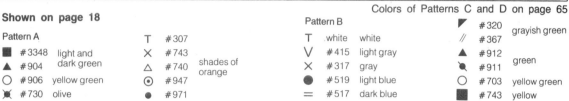

Shown on page 18

Pattern A

■	#3348	light and dark green	
▲	#904		
○	#906	yellow green	
✖	#730	olive	

T	#307	
✕	#743	
△	#740	shades of orange
⊙	#947	
●	#971	

Pattern B

T	.white	white
V	#415	light gray
✕	#317	gray
●	#519	light blue
=	#517	dark blue

Colors of Patterns C and D on page 65

◢	#320	grayish green
//	#367	
▲	#912	green
✎	#911	
○	#703	yellow green
■	#743	yellow

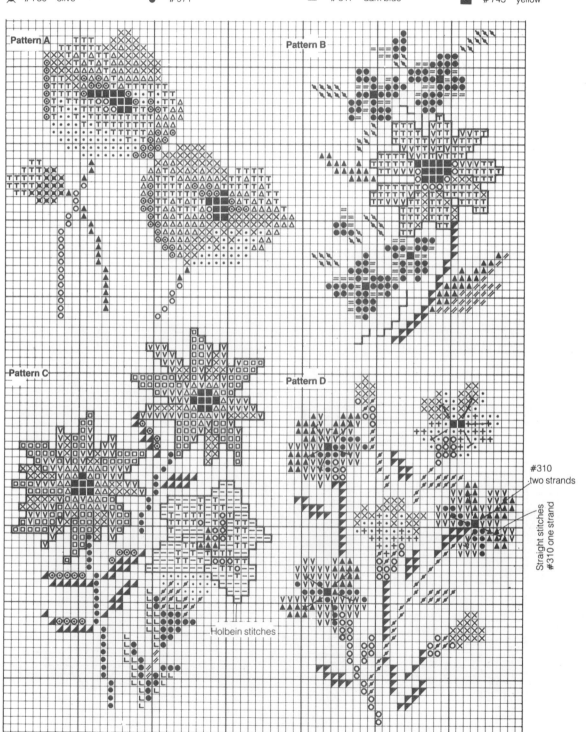

Pattern A

Pattern B

Pattern C

Pattern D

#310 two strands

Straight stitches #310 one strand

Holbein stitches

59

Shown on page 19

Pattern A

X #3689 — shades of pink
● #3687
// #3685
V #356 — red brown

■ #704
○ #703
T #913 — shades of green
— #911
⊙ #469
∕ #435 — light brown

Pattern B

∕ #800
● #809 — shades of blue
△ #798
□ white — white

◢ #320
// #470
● #469 — shades of green
— #319
○ #906

Pattern A

Pattern B

Pattern C

Pattern D

Straight stitches #310, two strands

Back stitches #913

60

V	#762	light and
X	#318	dark gray
■	#208	purple
✗	#744	cream
‖	#742	bright yellow

* Holbein stitches with two strands of gray #762

Pattern C

■	#826	light and
≫	#799	dark blue
V	#319	
O	#470	
▼	#368	
T	#913	shades of
△	#907	green
◢	#704	
⊙	#469	
—	#349	orangesh red
✗	#726	cream
‖	#742	bright yellow
●	#3689	pink
X	#762	silver gray
□	white	white

* Holbein stitches with two strands of yellowish red #349

Pattern D

╲	#601	shades of
+	#602	red violet
I	#603	
◥	#915	red violet
=	#726	cream
X	#742	bright yellow
⁒	#704	
▼	#469	shades of
●	#470	green
T	#937	
O	#906	

* Straight stitches with two strands of black #310

(Shown on page 20 to 23)

Doily

Materials: Java cloth fine weave white (#11) 40×40 cm; DMC embroidery thread size #25: one skein each of the colors for pattern C on page 62 and for pattern D below; white scalloped tape (5 mm wide) 150 cm; white bias tape 150 cm.
Finished size: See the diagram.

Instructions: Leave 9×9 squares in the center of the fabric and work pattern C as in the diagram below with four strands. Then work pattern D as in the diagram. Place the scalloped tape around the fabric, 37 cm in diameter, and hem with bias tape.

Centerpiece

Materials: Java cloth fine weave white (#11) 91×50 cm; DMC embroidery thread size #25: two skeins each of the colors for patterns A and B designated on pages 62 and 63.
Finished size: See the diagram.
Instructions: Work pattern A diagonally, as in the diagram below, with four strands.

Work 148 squares from the right bottom corner and the left top corner of pattern A, and continue the same patterns of the bud in the opposite end of pattern A, shown as ★ on the chart. Work pattern B three times. Hem the top and bottom of the fabric (3.5 cm) and make a fringe on the right and left sides of the fabric.

Pattern D

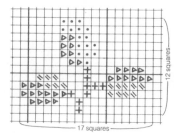

Diagram of finished doily

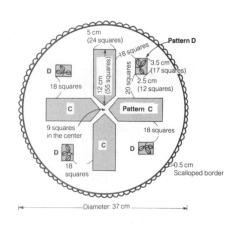

Diagram of finished centerpiece

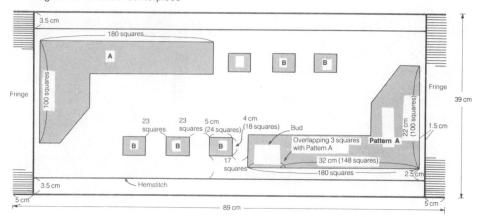

⊥ #957
□ #956
I #891
N #893 shades of pink
● #3689
> #3326
X #3329

+ #319
▷ #3346
— #3347
● #704 shades of green
◀ #906
○ #3343
< #368
⩘ #471

∫ #971
⤬ #743 shades of orange
⊣ #745
⊗ #607
■ #3053 light and dark olive
Z #3052

← Pattern C

Pattern B

Pattern shown as ★

⊙	#552		＼	#632	brown
∅	#915	shades of	S	#498	dark red
◣	#917	purple	●	#304	
⌐	#718				
☒	#502	grayish green			

Pattern A

★ Reduced 4 sqs. from 39 sqs. at the branch.

100 squares, Pattern A for centerpiece

184 squares Pattern A for centerpiece (152 sqs. +35 sqs. −overlapped 3 sqs.)

Pattern E

Pattern D

Pattern A

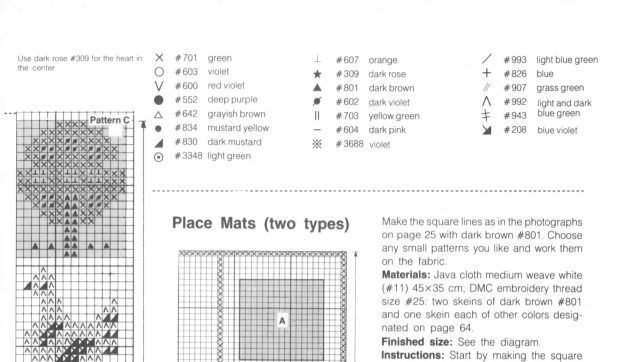

Use dark rose #309 for the heart in the center.

✕	#701	green	⊥	#607	orange
◯	#603	violet	★	#309	dark rose
V	#600	red violet	▲	#801	dark brown
●	#552	deep purple	✍	#602	dark violet
△	#642	grayish brown	‖	#703	yellow green
●	#834	mustard yellow	—	#604	dark pink
◢	#830	dark mustard	※	#3688	violet
⊙	#3348	light green			

/	#993	light blue green
+	#826	blue
//	#907	grass green
∧	#992	light and dark blue green
⨦	#943	
⊿	#208	blue violet

Place Mats (two types)

Make the square lines as in the photographs on page 25 with dark brown #801. Choose any small patterns you like and work them on the fabric.

Materials: Java cloth medium weave white (#11) 45×35 cm; DMC embroidery thread size #25: two skeins of dark brown #801 and one skein each of other colors designated on page 64.

Finished size: See the diagram.

Instructions: Start by making the square lines and then work the patterns. Hem the edges and complete. Use six strands for each color.

Patterns C and D shown on Page 18

Pattern C

☐	white	white
V	#415	light gray
✕	#317	gray
△	#727	pale yellow
■	#471	light green
T	#800	light blue
—	#334	blue
●	#312	dark blue
✍	#210	light purple
◯	#208	purple
▲	#307	yellow
//	#730	olive
L	#319	light and dark pale green
●	#367	
⊙	#597	green blue
◢	#992	dark green blue

Pattern D

■	#814	dark red
✕	#3689	
●	#3687	shades of violet
+	#3685	
●	#601	
▲	#3326	light and dark pink
V	#335	
✍	#3347	
◯	#469	shades of dark yellow green
◤	#3345	

Square Tablecloth

Materials: Java cloth medium weave white (#11) 90×140 cm one, 30×200 cm two, 30×90 cm two; DMC embroidery thread size #25: 15 skeins of violet #603, 8 skeins each of dark rose #309 and dark mustard yellow #730, 4 skeins each of other colors designated for the flower patterns in squares and for patterns A and B; cherry pink ribbon tape, (2 cm wide) 350 cm; green scalloped tape, (1.5 cm wide) 650 cm.

Finished size: See the diagram.

Instructions: Determine the center of the 90×140 cm fabric and work the patterns, referring to the diagram below, with six strands for each color. Cut the fabric to a size of 87×140 cm, attach fabric on all sides and turn the seams toward the outer edge. Hem the edges. Place the tape in an appropriate position and sew it. Sew the scalloped tape over the seams.

Finished diagram of square tablecloth

Scalloped tape (1.5 cm wide)

Tape (2 cm wide)

Seams

7 cm

Work the patterns here

42 cm (149 squares)

82 cm

82 cm

6 cm

6 cm

85 cm (309 squares)

7 cm

135 cm

22 cm

22 cm

Fold the hem twice and stitch by sewing machine.

24 cm

135 cm

24 cm

183 cm

Layout of the pattern

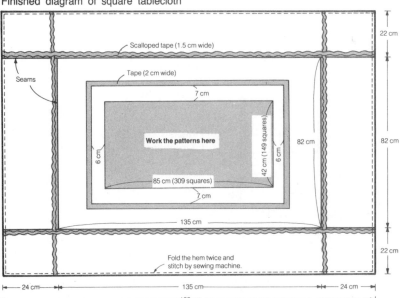

Center

B

A

B

A

74 squares

Flower pattern
43×39 squares

Flower pattern
43×39 squares

A   B   A   B   A   B

154 squares

Tea cozy

Materials: Java cloth Medium weave white (#11) two 30×30 cm; lining and kapoc 30×30 cm two of each; DMC embroidery thread size #25: one skein each of the colors for the flower in the center and patterns C, D, and E, 2 skeins of dark mustard yellow #730; cherry pink ribbon tape (2 cm wide) 70 cm.

Finished size: See the diagram.

Instructions: Work the patterns on the two fabrics, as in the diagram below, with 6 strands for each color. Sew together, with lining inside out, inserting a loop of ribbon tape at the top. Sew the ribbon tapes at the bottom as in the diagram and fill with kapoc to complete.

Diagrams of finished tea cozy

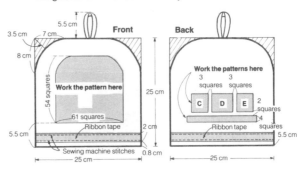

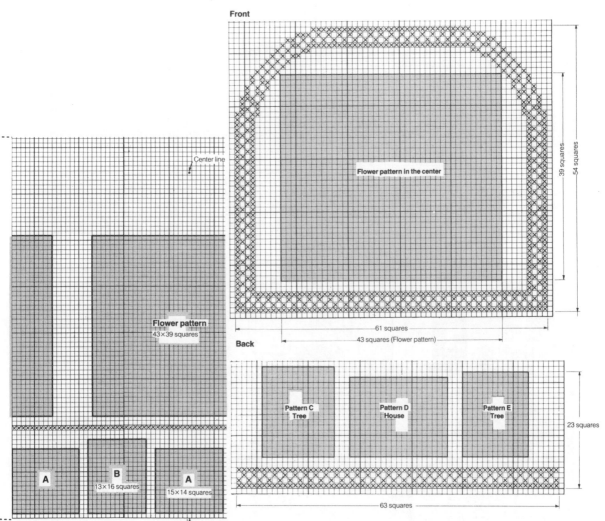

Tree Scenes

(Shown on pages 28 and 29)

Shown on page 28   / #839 dark brown   X #943 emerald green   I #445 yellow
                   ● #822 dove grey   ▲ #781 golden brown   ✳ #666 red

Holbein stitches with 4 strands

Holbein stitches with 4 strands

/ #839 dark brown ⊥ #3329 ☐ #553 light purple ○ #825 blue
✕ #700 shades of — #326 shades of | #3685 light and dark ● #807 light green blue
△ #702 green ℓ #309 rose red violet
! #704 // #899 ▲ #915 ■ #310 black

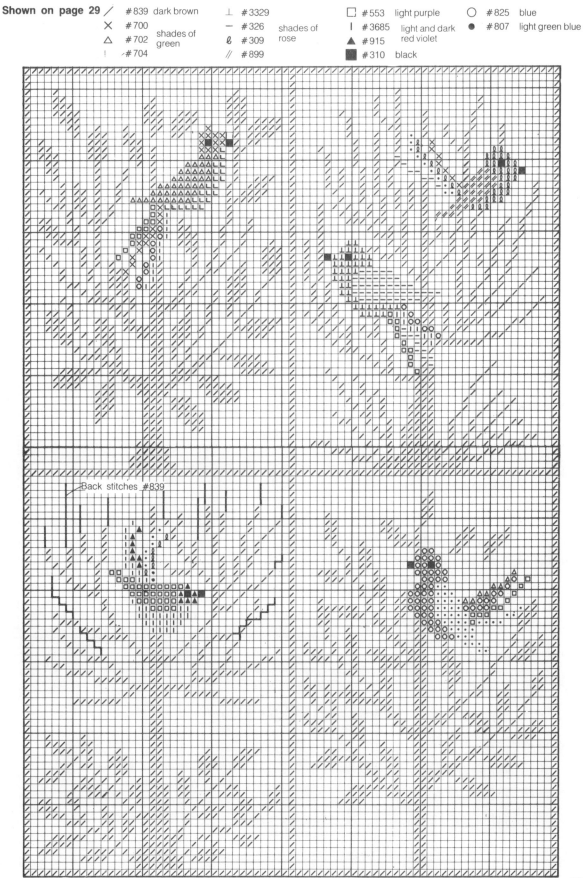

Back stitches #839

Cushions (three types)

Three types of cushions, with diffe-
rent layouts of the basic pattern.

Materials (for one): Java cloth Medium weave ivory #35 or rose red
#53 90×50 cm: Inner bag 90×50
cm; DMC embroidery thread size
#25; filling 400g; 30-cm zipper.
Finished size: See the diagram.
Instructions: Work the patterns using six strands for each color.

Embroidery threads for bedspread

+	#915 dark purple, 6 skeins	\\	#992 blue green, 6 skeins
×	#961 dark pink, 14 skeins	●	#209 light purple, 33 skeins
●	#963 pink, 6 skeins	.·	#208 dark purple, 6 skeins
		—	#209 purple, 6 skeins

Finished diagram
of bedspread.

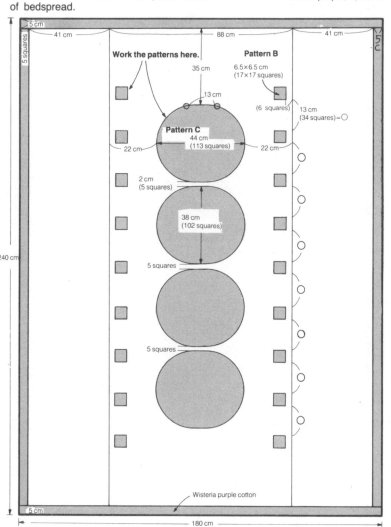

Work the patterns here.

Pattern B
6.5×6.5 cm
(17×17 squares)
(6 squares)

35 cm

13 cm

13 cm
(34 squares)=○

Pattern C
44 cm
(113 squares)

22 cm   22 cm

2 cm
(5 squares)

38 cm
(102 squares)

5 squares

5 squares

5 squares

41 cm   88 cm   41 cm

240 cm

180 cm

Wisteria purple cotton

5 cm

Bedspread

Materials: Java cloth large weave
ivory #35 90×480 cm; pink cotton for
lining 90×480 cm; DMC embroidery
thread size #25; wisteria cotton for
trimming 150×880 cm.
Finished size: See the diagram.
Instructions: Cut the fabric into a
90×240 cm and two 45×240 cm
sheets and sew them together as in
the diagram. Work the patterns, as in
the diagram, with 9 strands for each
color. Sew the lining, and hem the
edges with the wisteria cotton to
finish.

● See page 78 for embroidery
threads for cushions.

Diagram of finished cushions

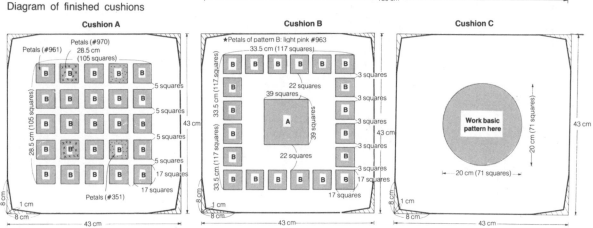

Cushion A

Petals (#961)
Petals (#970)
28.5 cm
(105 squares)

5 squares
5 squares
5 squares
5 squares
17 squares
17 squares

28.5 cm (105 squares)

Petals (#351)

43 cm

8 cm
1 cm
8 cm
43 cm

Cushion B

★Petals of pattern B: light pink #963
33.5 cm (117 squares)

3 squares
3 squares
22 squares
39 squares
3 squares
A
39 squares
3 squares
22 squares
3 squares
17 squares
17 squares

33.5 cm (117 squares)
33.5 cm (117 squares)

43 cm

8 cm
1 cm
8 cm
43 cm

Cushion C

Work basic
pattern here

20 cm (71 squares)

20 cm (71 squares)

43 cm

8 cm
1 cm
8 cm
43 cm

70

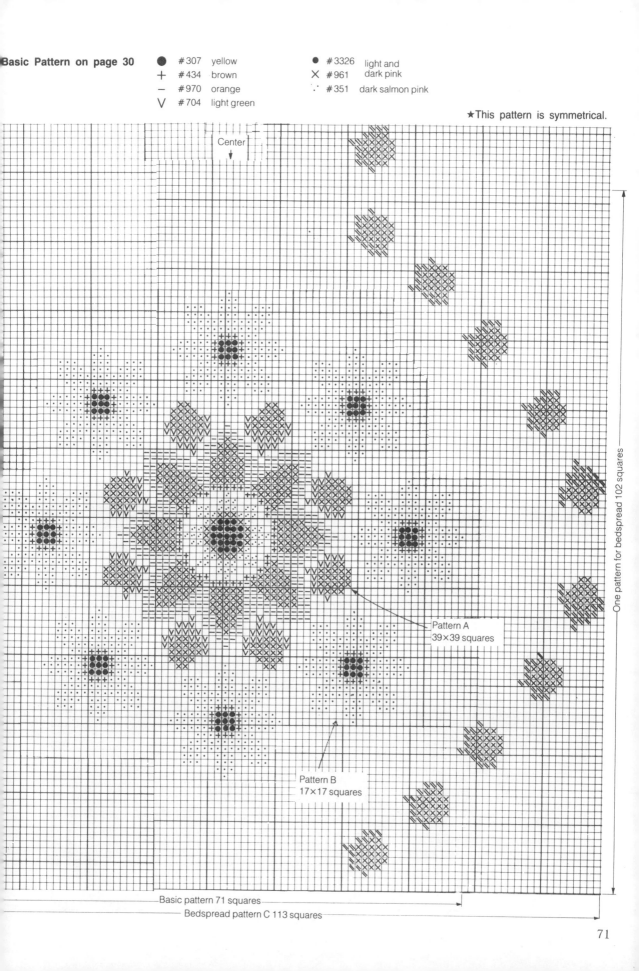

Basic Pattern on page 30

- ● #307 yellow
- + #434 brown
- − #970 orange
- V #704 light green
- ● #3326 light and
- X #961 dark pink
- ∴ #351 dark salmon pink

★This pattern is symmetrical.

Center

Pattern A
39×39 squares

Pattern B
17×17 squares

One pattern for bedspread 102 squares

Basic pattern 71 squares

Bedspread pattern C 113 squares

71

Birds and Berries

(Shown on pages 32 and 33)

Shown on page 32

△ #3348	∀ #632	
✕ #3345	∧ #407	shades of
◣ #3052	⊘ #921	brown
I #470	◢ #829	
⊠ #469	\ #301	
= #937 shades of		
− #935 green		
/ #3348		
⊿ #368		
● #503		
◑ #319		
φ #829		
▽ #498 light and dark		
‖ #814 wine red		

V #211	shades of	
+ #210	wisteria	
◤ #208		
◎ #792	pale blue	

☐ #922	light red brown
⊕ #725	pale yellow
● #712	ivory
▪ #829	olive

●• #349		
⊘ #352	shades of	
✳ #353	salmon pink	
■ #310	black	

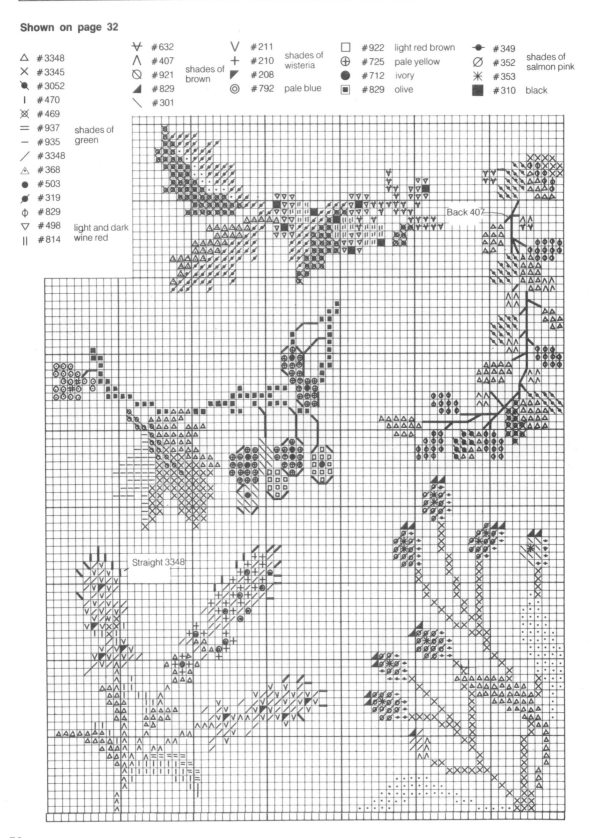

Back 407

Straight 3348

72

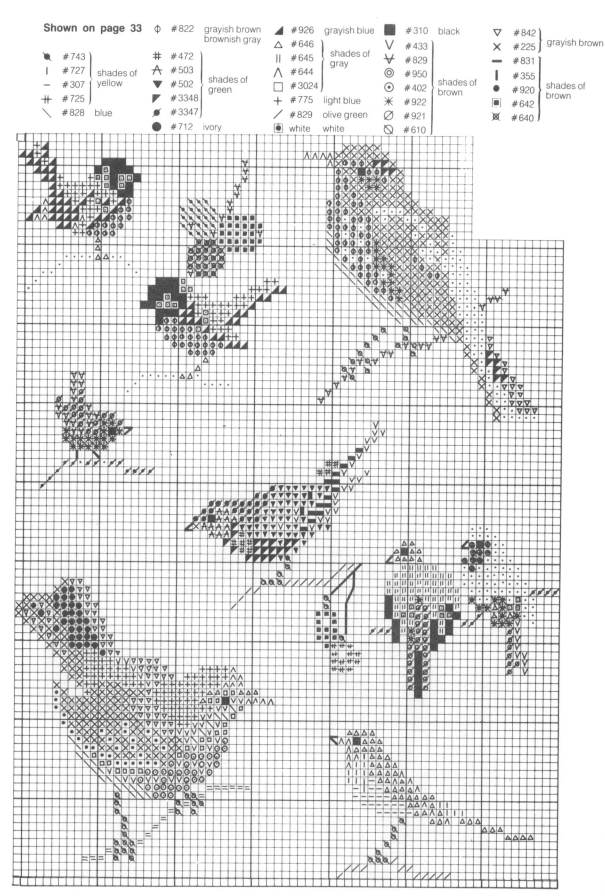

Shown on page 33

Symbol	Color No.	Color
●	#743	shades of yellow
I	#727	shades of yellow
–	#307	shades of yellow
‡‡	#725	shades of yellow
\	#828	blue
ɸ	#822	grayish brown brownish gray
#	#472	shades of green
A	#503	shades of green
▼	#502	shades of green
◤	#3348	shades of green
●	#3347	shades of green
●	#712	ivory
◢	#926	grayish blue
△	#646	shades of gray
‖	#645	shades of gray
Λ	#644	shades of gray
□	#3024	shades of gray
+	#775	light blue
/	#829	olive green
▣	white	white
■	#310	black
V	#433	shades of brown
∀	#829	shades of brown
◎	#950	shades of brown
⊙	#402	shades of brown
✳	#922	shades of brown
∅	#921	shades of brown
⦸	#610	shades of brown
▽	#842	grayish brown
×	#225	grayish brown
▬	#831	shades of brown
❙	#355	shades of brown
●	#920	shades of brown
▣	#642	shades of brown
⊠	#640	shades of brown

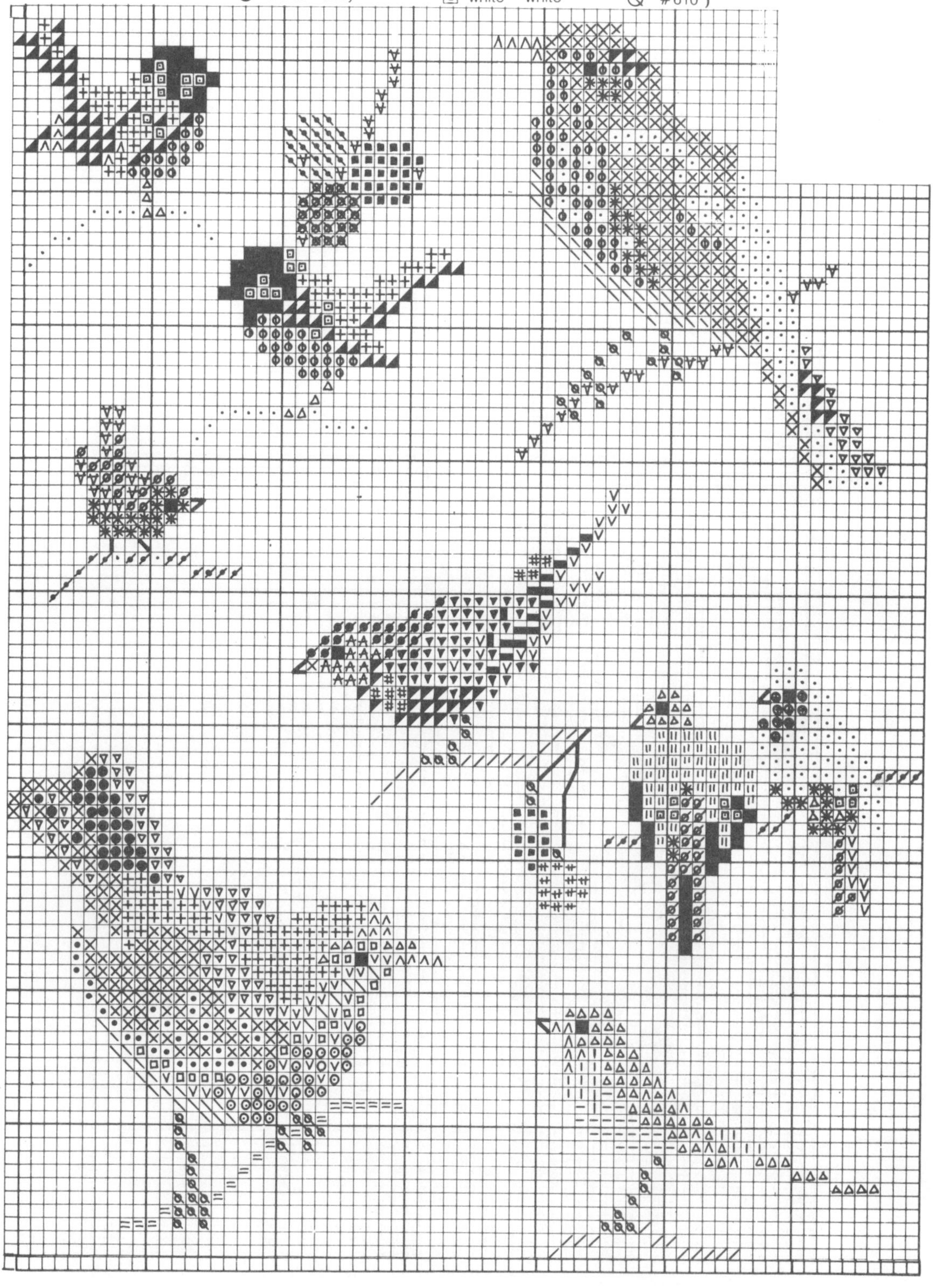

Birds and Flowers

(Shown on pages 34 and 35)

Shown on page 34

★These symbols are used in patterns A through F.

○ #666 red
● #3685 dark red violet
▼ #741 orange
+ #906 yellow green
× #327 purple
∨ #632 light brown
‖ #3687 light red violet
／ #518 light blue
● #208 blue purple

Pattern A
#666 red
#742 light orange
#741 orange
#906 yellow green
#3687 light red violet

Pattern B
#3685 dark red violet
#550 purple
#3687 violet

Pattern C
#741 orange
#3685 dark red violet
#3687 light red violet
#666 red

Pattern D
#208 wisteria purple
#518 light blue
#434 brown
#906 yellow green

Pattern E
#518 light blue
#517 blue
#3348 light yellow green

Pattern F
#208 blue violet
#518 light blue
#907 yellow green

74

Shown on page 35

V	#603	light red violet	\	#701 green
.˙	#917	violet	■	#208 wisteria purple
O	#666	red	T	#971 yellow orange
X	#838	dark brown	ø	#801 light brown
—	#725	yellow	●	#517 green blue
◣	#791	pale blue		

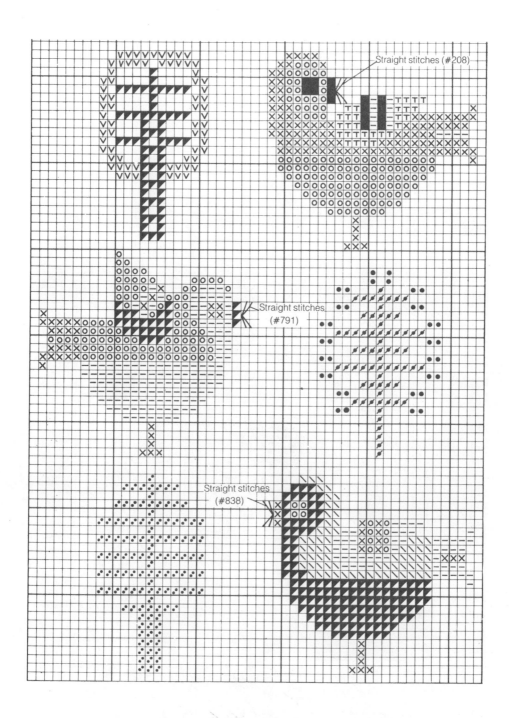

Straight stitches (#208)

Straight stitches (#791)

Straight stitches (#838)

(Shown on pages 36 and 37)

Shown on page 34

X #2154 gray
⊥ #743 bright yellow
○ #318 light gray
● #470 dark yellow green
╱ #825 blue
• #992 blue green
V #891 cherry pink

Shown on page 35

X #839 light brown
● #322
• #600 shades of
○ #601 red violet
■ #603 light indigo blue

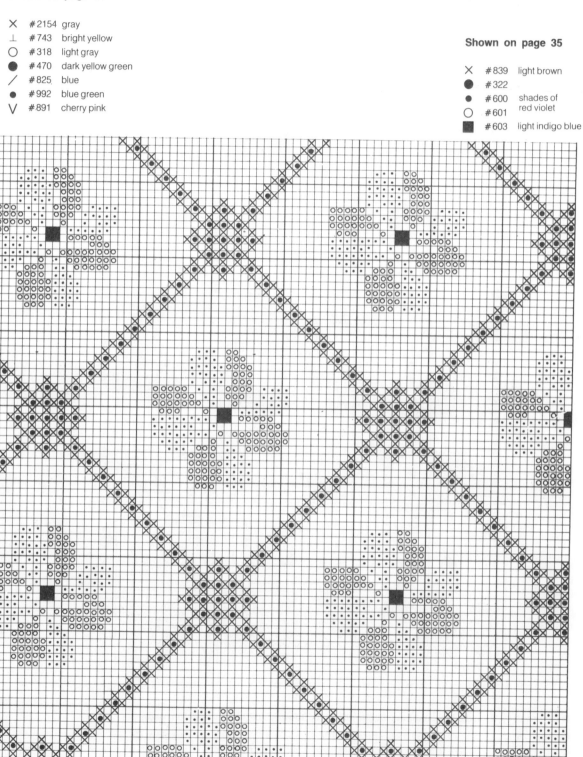

Tyrolean Patterns

(Shown on pages 38 and 39)

Shown on page 38

X	white	white
●	#666	red
V	#910	green
/	#725	yellow
Ø	#783	golden brown

● **Embroidery threads for cushions in the "Sweet Flowers" pattern shown on page 30.**

Cushion A:
five skeins of pink #3326, one skein each of yellow #307, brown #434, orange #970, and dark salmon pink #351.

Cushion B:
four skeins of light pink #963 for petals and one skein each of yellow #307, brown #434, and the other colors of the basic pattern.

Cushion C:
two skeins of pink #3326 and one skein each of colors for the basic pattern.

● #666 red   △ #632 light brown   ■ #801 dark brown
/ #962 pink   ● #742 bright yellow   ✳ #702 yellow green
∅ #996 light blue   ◢ #823 navy blue   ○ #829 olive
V #910 green   ✕ #312 blue

Straight stitches #666

Holbein stitches #801

742

Continuous Pattern of Birds and Flowers

(Shown on pages 40 and 41)

(Shown on pages 40 and 41)

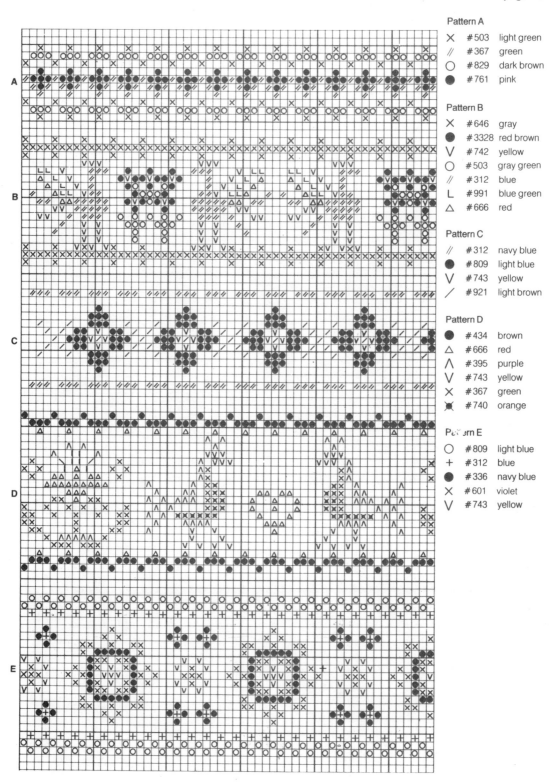

Shown on page 40

Pattern A

X	#503	light green
//	#367	green
O	#829	dark brown
●	#761	pink

Pattern B

X	#646	gray
●	#3328	red brown
V	#742	yellow
O	#503	gray green
//	#312	blue
L	#991	blue green
△	#666	red

Pattern C

//	#312	navy blue
●	#809	light blue
V	#743	yellow
/	#921	light brown

Pattern D

●	#434	brown
△	#666	red
Λ	#395	purple
V	#743	yellow
X	#367	green
✳	#740	orange

Pattern E

O	#809	light blue
+	#312	blue
●	#336	navy blue
X	#601	violet
V	#743	yellow

80

Pattern A

◣ #3689   light red brown
◯ #647   light brown

Pattern B

∨ #775   light blue
▲ #322   blue
✕ #307   yellow

Pattern C

∅ #437   light brown
⊘ #838   dark brown
⊗ #504   gray green

Pattern D

● #605   purple pink
◯ #367   dark green
✕ #963   pink

Pattern E

T #552   purple
// #334   blue

Pattern F

✕ #307   yellow
+ #741   orange
⊥ #471   yellow green

Pattern G

∧ #700   green
+ #741   orange
△ #666   red

Pattern H

※ #936   green brown
◉ #760   peach pink
∅ #437   light brown

Pattern I

+ #741   orange yellow
⊃ #743   orange
◢ #966   light green
✕ #3047   cream

Pattern J

◼ #335   dark pink
⊥ #907   yellow green
⊐ #894   pink
   #383   light brown

Pattern K

// #775   light blue
∨ #334   blue
◯ #700   green
✕ #322   dark blue

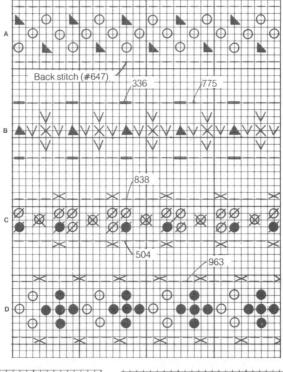

Back stitch (#647)   336   775

838

504

963

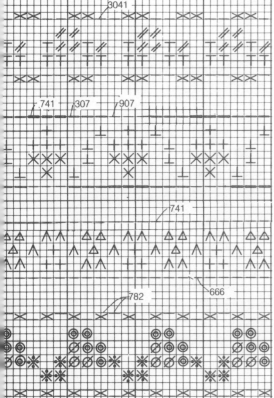

3041

741   307   907

741

782   666

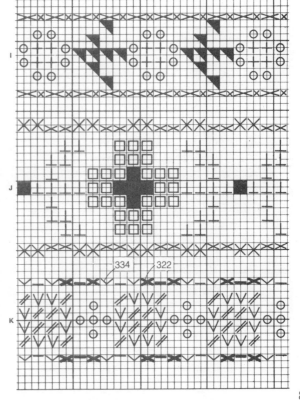

334   322

Camellia

(Shown on page 42)

Bag

Materials: Java cloth medium weave light brown (#52) 55 x 30 cm; cotton for lining 55×30 cm; brown round cord (of any material) 60 cm×2; DMC embroidery thread size #25: one skein each of the 13 colors for the pattern and 4 skeins of yellow brown #434.

Finished size: See the diagram.

Instructions: Work the patterns of the fabric with 6 strands for each color. Complete the bag, making eight loops for the cords.

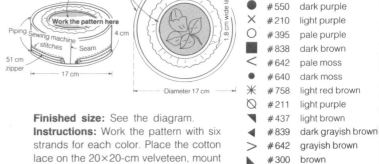

Diagram of finished pouch bag

Pouch

Materials: Java cloth medium weave light brown (#52) 15×15 cm; gray velveteen 20×20 cm, two; cotton lining 20×20 cm, two (top & bottom); and 7×56 cm (side); velveteen for piping, 1.5×60 cm, two, and 1.5×40 cm, one; DMC embroidery thread size #25: one skein each of the colors for the flower pattern, and yellow brown #434 for the background; light gray cotton lace, (2.5-cm wide) 100 cm; 51-cm zipper.

Finished size: See the diagram.

Instructions: Work the pattern with six strands for each color. Place the cotton lace on the 20×20-cm velveteen, mount the embroidered fabric on it and finish with the piping. Attach the lining, and complete the pouch.

\	white	white
●	#550	dark purple
×	#210	light purple
○	#395	pale purple
■	#838	dark brown
<	#642	pale moss
●	#640	dark moss
✳	#758	light red brown
⊘	#211	light purple
◤	#437	light brown
◀	#839	dark grayish brown
>	#642	grayish brown
◣	#300	brown

★ Background in yellow brown #434 around the pattern.

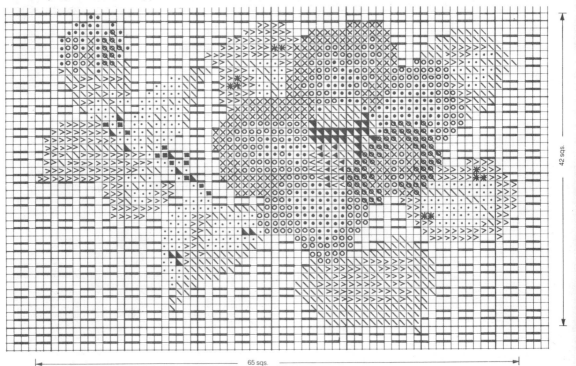

65 sqs.

42 sqs.